Discussion Paper

80

THE RUSSIAN FAR EAST

Prospects for the New Millennium

Michael Bradshaw

THE ROYAL INSTITUTE OF
INTERNATIONAL AFFAIRS

THE RUSSIAN FAR EAST
Prospects for the New Millennium

Michael Bradshaw

**THE ROYAL INSTITUTE OF
INTERNATIONAL AFFAIRS
Russia and Eurasia Programme**

© Royal Institute of International Affairs, 1999

Published in Great Britain in 1999 by the Royal Institute of International Affairs,
Chatham House, 10 St James's Square, London SW1Y 4LE (Charity Registration No. 208 223)

ISBN 1 86203 073 1

Printed and bound in Great Britain by Selwood Printing Ltd

*The Royal Institute of International Affairs publishes RIIA
Discussion Papers to make research results, policy discussions and
important background information available as speedily as possible
and in a concise manner to those concerned with international
policy issues. The series thus provides summaries of work that may
subsequently be published in a more substantial form.*

*The Royal Institute of International Affairs, at Chatham House in
London, has provided an independent forum for discussion and
debate on current international issues for nearly 80 years. Its
resident research fellows, specialized information resources, and
range of publications, conferences and meetings span the fields of
international politics, economics and security. The Institute does not
express opinions of its own; the views expressed in this publication
are the responsibility of the author.*

CONTENTS

ABOUT THE AUTHOR

Michael Bradshaw is an associate fellow within the Russia and Eurasia Programme of the Royal Institute of International Affairs. He is a senior lecturer in the School of Geography and Environmental Sciences and an associate member of the Centre for Russian and East European Studies at the University of Birmingham. Among his publications are *Russia's Regions: A Business Analysis* (London: EIU, 1996) and *Geography and Transition in the Post-Soviet Republics* (Chichester: J. Wiley & Sons, 1997).

ACKNOWLEDGMENTS

This study has been prepared within the framework of a three-and-a-half-year research project funded by the Economic and Social Research Council (ESRC) as part of its Pacific-Asia Programme (grant no. L324253005). I am also grateful for the support of Dr Roy Allison, Head of the Russia and Eurasia Programme at the Royal Institute of International Affairs, who suggested that this analysis, which started life as an internal RIIA briefing document, be published as a discussion paper and obtained the necessary funds for this purpose. I would like to thank Rachel Jenkins, also of the Russia and Eurasia Programme, for all her help in organizing the Russian Far East seminar at Chatham House in September 1998. Finally, I wish to thank the Russian Far East Advisory Group LLC (Seattle) for allowing me to reproduce their map of the Russian Far East.

December 1998   M.B.

SUMMARY

This paper presents a study of the current economic and political situation in the Russian Far East. The study examines how the Soviet system created a highly distorted and dependent peripheral economy in the Far East. The region's current economic problems are a direct consequence of that legacy. In the post-Soviet period the region has sought to expand its trade relations with the Asia-Pacific region. The study identifies the key trade partners, considers the various political factors influencing the trade and development relationship and assesses the role of foreign trade and investment in the region. The final chapter identifies the key determinants of growth and presents a number of scenarios for the future development of the Russian Far East.

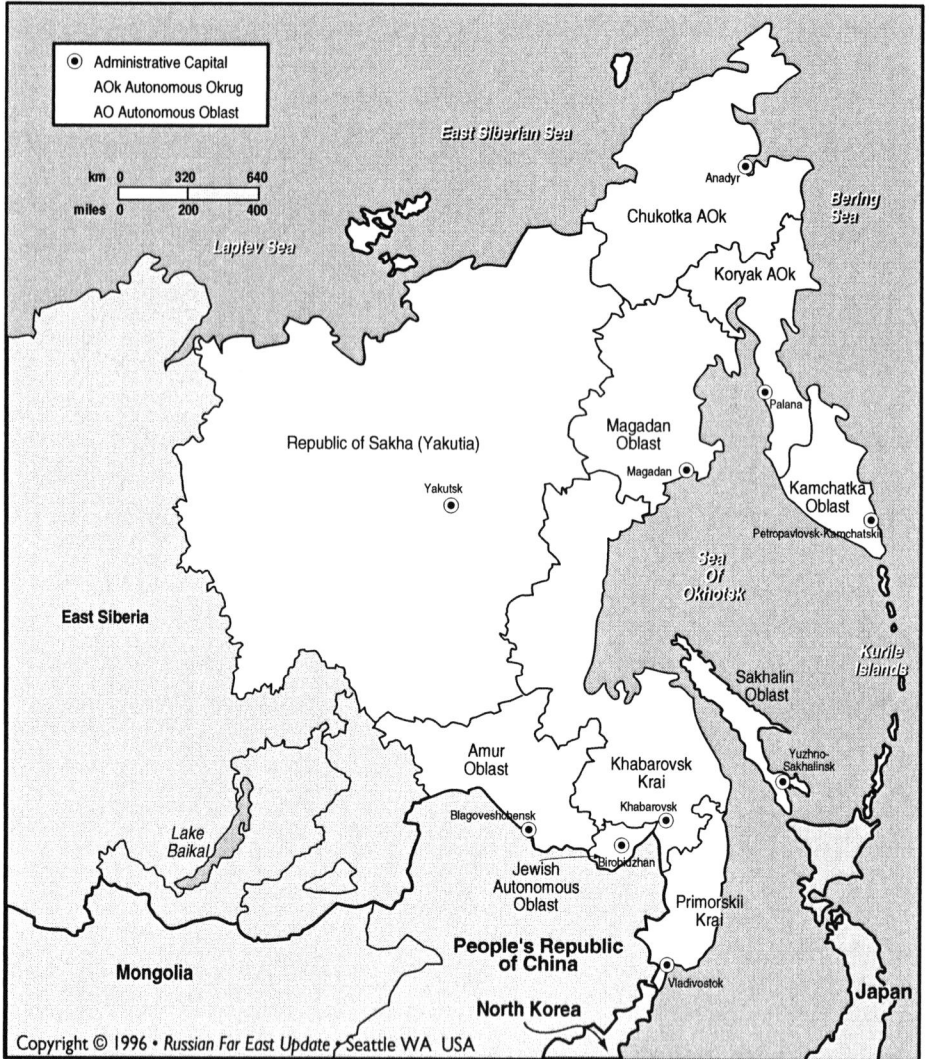

The Russian Far East

INTRODUCTION

The Russian Far East defined

The subject of this discussion paper is the Russian Far East (hereafter RFE).[1] The RFE has no legal administrative status in the Russian Federation. The region of the RFE, as defined in Table 1 and illustrated in the map opposite, has its origins in a system of economic planning regions devised by Gosplan USSR. These regions were used for strategic long-term planning during the Soviet period. Nonetheless, they have come to take on an identity of their own. Politicians, planners and the population of Russia also recognize these regions and they have served as the focus for the development of interregional economic associations, such as the Inter-regional Association for Economic Cooperation of the Russian Far East and Trans-baykal (previously the Far Eastern Economic Association). The RFE is composed of ten separate administrative units, or federal subjects, that are recognized by the Federal Constitution; however, these ten units occupy varying positions within Russia's federal structure. They account for 36.4 per cent of the territory of the Russian Federation, 5.1 per cent of its population and, in 1995, 5.8 per cent of Russia's gross regional product.

Although the Russian Constitution deems all federal subjects to be equal, the reality is somewhat different. The republics within the federation, whose name reflects the existence of particular ethnic groups, have seized greater autonomy. Thus, the Republic of Sakha (Yakutia) has negotiated a special relationship with the federal government and has greater autonomy than the other regions within the RFE. The asymmetrical nature of Russian federalism also helps to explain the relative weakness of interregional alliances in Russia. For most regions, so far at least, the most important political and economic relationship is their relationship with Moscow. This explains why some of the lower order administrative units, which were previously subordinate to an oblast or krai, have declared themselves to be independent units in their own right. Thus, the Chukotka Autonomous Okrug has separated from Magadan Oblast and the Jewish Autonomous Oblast has separated from Khabarovsk Krai. As autonomous units, a definition which again relates to the presence of distinct ethnic groups, these regions are granted certain privileges not bestowed upon 'ordinary' oblasts and krais. For the purpose of the current analysis

1

Table 1: Characteristics of the administrative regions of the Russian Far East

	Territory '000 km²	Total population ('000s) I Jan 1997	Population density persons per km²	Regional capital	% of population living in urban areas
Russia	107075.4	147502	8.6		73.1
RFE	6215.9	7421	1.2		75.7
Sakha (Yakutia)	3103.2	1016	0.3	Yakutsk	64.3
Jewish Aut. Oblast	36.0	207	5.7	Birobidzhan	67.5
Chukotka Aut. Okrug	737.7	85	0.1	Anadyr	69.8
Primorskii Krai	165.9	2236	13.5	Vladivostok	78.1
Khabarovsk Krai	788.6	1557	2.0	Khabarovsk	80.5
Amur Oblast	363.7	1031	2.8	Blagoveshchensk	64.5
Kamchatka Oblast	472.3	404	0.9	Petropavlovsk-Kamchatskii	80.8
Koryak Aut. Okrug	301.5	32	0.1	Palana	24.9
Magadan Oblast	461.4	251	0.6	Magadan	90.0
Sakhalin Oblast	87.1	634	7.3	Yuzhno-Sakhalinsk	86.1

Source: Goskomstat Rossii, *Demographic Yearbook of Russia, 1997* (Goskomstat: Moscow, 1997), pp. 15–29.

it is sufficient to recognize that the RFE comprises ten administrative units, one of which is a republic. The real nature of any individual region's relationship with Moscow, and thus its place in the federal hierarchy, is determined by bargaining between the centre and the regions. Numerous regions have signed 'power-sharing agreements' with Moscow that divide rights and responsibilities between the federal government and the regional administration. This makes it impossible to generalize about the true nature of centre–region relations in the RFE, or anywhere else in Russia for that matter.

If the internal structure of the RFE were not confusing enough, matters are further complicated by the fact that the federal government's 'Programme for the Economic and Social Development of the Far East and Transbaykal 1996–2005' refers to a region that is bigger than the RFE as conventionally defined. Three regions which are normally considered part of the East Siberian economic region, the Republic of Buryatia, Chita Oblast and the Aga-Buryat Autonomous Okrug (which is subordinate to Chita) are included as the 'Transbaykal'. This larger region accounts for 40.9 per cent of Russia's territory, but only 6.7 per cent of its population and 7 per cent of its gross regional product. This area, which is basically all of Russia east of Lake Baykal, is sometimes referred to as Pacific Russia. Although it is a significant share of Russian territory and of considerable strategic significance, it is not at present a vital component of the Russian economy and is some considerable distance from the political and economic core of the country in European Russia. The current analysis focuses upon the administrative units of the RFE; however, the larger region of Pacific Russia, which may even include Irkutsk Oblast, needs to be considered in relation to federal policy. As we shall see, this is rather academic: the federal government cannot afford to implement its development programme anyway![2]

From collapse to crisis

The decade of the 1990s is likely to go down in the history of the RFE as a particularly difficult period. Even prior to the collapse of the Soviet Union, in the late 1980s, the region was starting to show signs of economic stress. The policies of perestroika had turned attention towards the modernization of the economy of European Russia and away from the resource-producing regions of Siberia and the Far East. This happened at a time when the economy in the RFE was in need of fresh investment to modernize and develop new resources. During the 1970s billions had been wasted on the construction of the Baykal Amur Mainline (BAM) railway, and the hoped-for resource boom, which would have brought that investment, failed to materialize. Thus, as the Soviet system started to collapse, the economy of the RFE was far from internationally competitive and was in desperate need of substantial capital investment. Even during the Soviet period it was hoped that the supposed complementarity between the resource-rich RFE and the resource-poor nations of Northeast Asia, principally Japan, would promote trade and investment. This has turned out to be largely illusory. Transitional recession has compromised the resource base of the RFE, and international competition, and now recession, has reduced the short-term demand for resources in Northeast Asia. This is not to say that there has not been an increase in economic interaction between the RFE and Northeast Asia; as we shall see, there has. However, the anticipated inward investment has, with a few notable exceptions, failed to materialize. Thus, the RFE finds itself in the unenviable position of having tied itself to Northeast Asia to overcome the problems of economic collapse in Russia, only to find Asia facing economic crisis. The current economic crisis in Russia must seem the final straw – having failed to attract investment from Asia, the RFE now recognizes that Moscow cannot provide the kind of support needed to bring about economic recovery. Furthermore, Moscow's failure, so far, to create a stable environment for foreign investors makes it very difficult for the RFE to persuade multinational companies to help develop the region's resource potential.

Structure of the analysis

The aims of this study are to assess the current situation in the RFE and to present a number of scenarios for the future development of the region. To achieve these aims, the study is divided into five major sections. Chapter 2 considers the impact of the Soviet system upon the RFE. It is shown that the region has inherited a distorted economic structure and a high degree of dependence upon external suppliers. Chapter 3 examines the economic problems created by those legacies and the impact that they are having upon the region. Chapter 4 examines the political relationships that have developed in the post-Soviet period, both domestic and international. This is then followed, in Chapter 5, by analysis of the role of foreign trade and investment in the economy of the RFE. The final chapter identifies the key determinants of growth as a means of building three scenarios for future development: boom, bust and muddling through. The conclusion reflects on the current position of the RFE and the short-term prospects.

2 THE SOVIET LEGACY

Many of the economic problems that now face the RFE are a direct result of the priorities of Moscow during the Soviet period and the role that the region played in the centrally planned economy. To understand the current socio-economic situation it is therefore necessary to assess the impact of the Soviet legacy as this constrains what is possible today and in the short term.

The making of a resource periphery

The Soviet system produced a very 'narrow' economic structure in the RFE. The emphasis was upon resource development, principally for the needs of the national economy (Table 2 compares the branch structure of industrial production in the RFE with that of Russia). The degree of economic specialization was even more extreme in the northern regions. For example, in Sakha and Magadan the mining industry has accounted for over 60 per cent of industrial production and this degree of specialization has actually increased since the break-up of the Soviet Union.[3]

Because of the region's remoteness from the European core region, a great deal of economic effort was expended on transportation. Most of the machinery and equipment needed by the region's industries and the food and consumer goods required by the population were imported from the western regions of the Soviet Union. In the late Soviet period inshipments into the RFE exceeded outshipments 1.8 times by value and 2.5 times by volume. The region imported 95 per cent of products of ferrous metallurgy, 80 per cent of those of the chemical industry, 70–80 per cent of light industry and over 50 per cent of machine-building products from elsewhere in the Soviet Union.[4] Equally, the market for the region's industrial goods and food products (fish) was the western region of the country. This 'shuttle' of goods to and fro was possible because the Soviet system did not account for the cost of transportation.

The geostrategic role of the RFE further aggravated the attitude of 'development regardless of cost'. The ports of Vladivostok and Petropavlovsk-Kamchatka, for example, were key to the Pacific Fleet and the Soviet Union's power projection into Northeast Asia and the Pacific Ocean; the border regions with China were highly

5

Table 2: Branch structure of industrial production in 1995

Branch	Russia	RFE	LQ
Electric power generation	13.5	19.3	1.4
Fuel	16.4	10.5	0.6
Ferrous metals	9.1	0.5	0.1
Non-ferrous metals	6.5	20.7	3.2
Chemicals and petrochemicals	7.5	0.7	0.1
Machine-building and metal-working	17.9	8.5	0.5
Wood, cellulose and paper	5.1	5.4	1.1
Building materials	4.8	4.0	0.8
Glass and ceramic	0.3	0.2	0.7
Light	2.5	0.6	0.2
Food*	12.1	25.3	2.1
Flour milling and mixed fodder	2.1	2.0	0.9

*Includes the fishing industry.
LQ = Location Quotient; a figure greater than 1 indicates a level of specialization above the national average.

Source: Goskomstat Rossii, *Rossiyskiy Statisticheskiy Ezhegodnik* (Moscow: Goskomstat, 1995).

militarized as were the Kurile Islands (Northern Territories); the mining activities in the region (particularly in the far north) were crucial to maintaining self-sufficiency in strategic minerals and metals; and finally, the expansion of the Northern-Sea Route was seen as a key component of the effective occupation of the Arctic. All of these activities required the development of a substantial socio-economic infrastructure, the sustainability of which was way beyond the means of the region's economy. As Leslie Dienes noted:

> This subordinate, dependent relationship with the rest of the country is shown even more clearly by the huge volume of interregional subsidy flowing into the Far East and Transbaykalia. Through the vast area east of Lake Baykal, a full third of the regional income utilized during the mid-1970s was subsidy from other regions of the country.[5]

Export-oriented development

Despite its geostrategic role, according to official statements, the RFE was just about the only region in the Soviet Union where the promotion of an export-based development strategy was pursued. Thus, during the 1970s and 1980s the region was supposed to have benefited from expanded trade with the Asia-Pacific region (hereafter APR). The reality was somewhat different. In fact, most of Moscow's trade with the APR was economic support for client states such as Vietnam, Cambodia and Laos and involved commodities that were not produced in the RFE.[6] Thus, the RFE contributed less than a third of the Soviet Union's trade with the APR, and most of that trade was with Japan. Moreover, Moscow continued to exercise central control over foreign trade. Only a small amount of local trade was permitted through *Dal'intorg* (the regional foreign trade organization that controlled border trade). The creation of a number of large-scale, long-term compensation agreements between Japan and the Soviet Union formed the centrepiece of this export-based strategy.[7] The resources of the RFE were mortgaged to finance the purchase of machinery and equipment for resource development. These agreements were important in developing the South Yakutian Coal Complex and in delineating the oil and gas deposits offshore of Sakhalin. They also financed the development of the Vostochnii port at Nakhodka. In the forestry sector they resulted in exports of logs and woodchips, but did not promote the expansion of the forest products industry. Thus, these agreements helped establish the RFE's role as a potential supplier of natural resources to the APR. They also created the expectation that foreign governments (principally Japan) would finance large-scale, long-term resource development projects.

A dependent periphery

At the end of the Soviet period the RFE exhibited all the characteristics of a resource-periphery locked into a colonial relationship with the economic core of European Russia. It had a 'truncated' economic structure, heavily biased towards resource production and dependent upon the core for manufactured and consumer goods, and which required substantial financial assistance to maintain its socio-economic infrastructure. The region's manufacturing industry was oriented to the needs of the military-industrial complex (VPK) and not the resource sector.[8] Furthermore, that military activity demanded a level of infrastructure provision which the region could not support. Moscow provided substantial economic assistance because of the region's geostrategic significance and paid little attention to the long-term economic viability of the region's economy.

A recent study by the Australian government's East Asian Analytical Unit aptly describes the current plight of the RFE.

> For decades, Pacific Russia's economic growth was based largely on Moscow's desire to develop the region for defence and strategic reasons. A wide range of subsidies and other forms of economic support were provided by Moscow to develop industries and attract personnel to the region. When these supports were removed by reforms and the collapse of the USSR, Pacific Russia's economy was virtually cut adrift.[9]

3 THE CURRENT SOCIO-ECONOMIC SITUATION

Given what has been said above, it is easy to see why the collapse of the Soviet Union has brought economic crisis to the RFE. Simply put, the region has inherited a level of economic activity that it cannot currently sustain. Moreover, the distorted structure and dependent nature of the regional economy have left the RFE totally unprepared for market-type reform. Unfortunately, it has proved to be the case that despite the rhetoric the federal government in Moscow has neither the funds nor the inclination to assist the region. Thus, a certain amount of downsizing and restructuring was inevitable. However, the specific nature of Russia's economic transition and the specific policies of the federal government have actually aggravated the situation and many parts of the RFE now face economic collapse. Even so, it is important to note that any assessment of the RFE must acknowledge the substantial variations that exist within the region. One cannot really talk of a coherent RFE economy as each region faces a different set of problems. The major socio-economic problems facing the region are discussed in more detail below.

Industrial decline

The entire Russian economy has experienced a substantial decline in industrial production. According to official statistics, at the end of 1995 the value of industrial production in Russia was 49.9 per cent of the level it had been in 1991 (see Table 3). These same figures suggest that the RFE actually fared better than many regions in Russia. This is because of the region's reliance upon resource industries, which did not suffer as much as the machine-building industries.

However, it is clear that those regions of the RFE that did have a more balanced economy (i.e. more machine-building) have experienced more substantial industrial decline – this is true of both Primorskii and Khabarovsk Krais, where 51 per cent of the region's population reside. The apparent resilience of the RFE industrial base is largely illusory. This is because the data are based on the value of production and reflect the fact that resource prices have rapidly increased to world levels. Thus, physical volume has declined much faster than the value of production. Unfortunately, the

Table 3: Percentage economic decline in the Russian Far East, 1990–95

	Industrial production	Economically active	Industrial workforce	Atmospheric emissions (from stationary sources)	Electricity generation	Unemployd as % econ. active in 1995
Russia	-50	-11.8	-4.4	-37.5	-20.5	3.2
RFE	-54	-15.9	-3.0	-42.9	-18.9	n.d.
Sakha	-25	-10.0	-0.9	-37.5	-15.3	0.8
Primorskii	-44	-10.4	-6.1	-45.1	-25.4	3.0
Khabarovsk	-67	-17.4	-3.1	-52.1	-18.5	5.3
Amur	-53	-6.9	-2.9	-38.4	-12.8	5.5
Kamchatka	-53	-16.2	1.0	-4.6	-15.8	4.6
Magadan	-39	-42.2	0.7	-38.3	-20.5	2.6
Sakhalin	-42	-26.6	1.8	-46.1	-20.6	5.4

Note: Disaggregated data for the Jewish Autonomous Oblast and Chukotka are not available; they are included in the statistics for Khabarovsk and Magadan respectively, except in the case of the data on decline in industrial production, which omit these two regions. Koryak is included, as is usual, in Kamchatka.

Source: Goskomstat Rossii, *Regiony Rossii, Tom 1* (Goskomstat: Moscow, 1997) and Goskomstat Rossii, *Rossiyskiy Statisticheskiy Ezhegodnik* (Logos: Moscow, 1996).

recent declines in world commodity prices have further depressed the profitability of enterprises in the RFE. For example, the region's only oil producer Rosneft'-Sakhalinmorneftgaz now faces severe economic difficulties due to rising production costs, stagnant production and depressed oil prices.

Table 3 shows that the size of the industrial workforce fell by only 3 per cent, while other measures of decline suggest a much more significant level of industrial decline. Physical measures of production, particularly in the fuels–energy complex, show substantial declines. Equally, official unemployment remains high despite substantial out-migration. A further indicator of decline is that the atmospheric emissions from stationary sources (such as power stations and factories) fell by 43 per cent between 1990 and 1995.

The structural consequence of differential industrial declines has been an increasing reliance upon the resource sectors of the economy. The machine-building (including VPK) and resource-processing industries, which are concentrated in the south, have collapsed, but the resource-producing sectors continue to operate, though at reduced levels. In 1990 the fuels, non-ferrous, timber and timber products branches accounted for 32.4 per cent of the value of industrial output in the RFE. By 1995 that share had increased to 36.6 per cent. At the same time, the share of the machine-building and metalworking branches declined from 15.3 per cent to 8.5 per cent. The resource industries of the north are capital-intensive and tend to employ fewer people than the manufacturing industries in the south. While there has been some service-sector growth, it has been concentrated in the southern cities of Khabarovsk and Vladivostok and cannot provide new jobs for workers laid off in the one-industry settlements in the more remote regions of the RFE.

Economic transition has brought with it inflation and increased production costs. In part, this reflects an adjustment to more 'realistic' pricing levels after the 'distortions' of the Soviet system. In the RFE two aspects of production costs are particularly significant: energy and transportation costs. Both have increased dramatically during the post-Soviet period. For example, the share of transport costs in the production of metal products in the RFE has increased from 2.4 per cent in 1991 to 18–22 per cent in 1995. Increasing transportation costs have cut off the region's industries from their traditional markets in European Russia. More generally, increased costs have reduced the profitability of industry in the region, which has resulted in major financial problems. Because of continued subsidy, the region has yet to feel the impact of the 'real' cost of energy production. Should the high cost of local energy production be passed on to industry and households in the RFE there will be further economic hardship and reductions in profitability. The latest economic crisis, caused by the collapse of the rouble, can only bring further economic hardship to the region as the majority of foodstuffs and luxury goods are now imported from abroad. The collapse of the rouble is even affecting Chinese border traders, as they prefer to change roubles into dollars before taking their profits back to China. Now the roubles earned will not even cover their costs. There is now real concern that this winter will bring starvation and disease as the local populace simply lacks the money to buy all but the most basic provisions.

Payments problems and economic crisis

Increasing costs and declining profitability have already generated a substantial non-payments crisis in the RFE. Enterprises have no money to pay either their bills or their workforce. Equally they are unable to pay their taxes, both federal and local. This has resulted in major problems in the region's energy complex.[10] Consumers are not paying their electricity bills, with the result that the power generators are not paying the coalmines, which in turn are not paying their workers. As a result the mines stop deliveries and generators cut supplies. The local administration is unable to break this vicious circle because its tax base has also been compromised by the non-payments crisis. When the federal government provides funds to resolve the problem they are often misused by the local administrations (this is particularly problematic in Primorskii Krai). In any event, they simply lubricate the system for a while and do nothing to solve the structural origins of the problem. In the summer of 1998 coal miners on Sakhalin brought the island to a virtual standstill as they blockaded the railway line to the main power station in Yuzhno-Sakhalinsk. The mining companies and utility companies are caught in a situation in which they have no funds to invest in new capacity and equipment, and thus the longer-term sustainability of the energy system is threatened. Equally, outside investors are unlikely to be attracted to such a situation. Only substantial federal investment to modernize the coalmines and power stations can ease the short-term crisis. In the long term the delivery of gas from Sakhalin should provide the RFE with a cheap and clean source of energy for heating and electricity generation. The federal government has devised a gasification plan for the southern regions of the RFE, but it is difficult to see where the funding will come from. Furthermore, the governors of Khabarovsk and Sakhalin are arguing over whether the priority should be first to deliver gas to the mainland or to pipe it to the south of the island of Sakhalin.

Declining living standards

The social consequence of industrial decline, increasing costs and the payments problem is a decline in living standards. Wages and the cost of living in the RFE have always been higher than the national average. During the Soviet period much of the region's workforce was eligible for 'northern increments'. At the same time consumer goods were supplied at subsidized prices, and special privileges such as cheap travel were granted. Now these subsidies and privileges have disappeared and the cost of living has increased accordingly. Increased transport costs have cut off the regions from Russian suppliers, and traders have turned to the import of food and consumer goods from neighbouring countries in Northeast Asia. Until recently, there was not so much a shortage of goods (although this was very much a problem in the more remote regions) as a shortage of consumers with purchasing power. Official statistics suggest that wages are substantially higher than the national average, but the cost of living is even higher. Furthermore, because of the non-payments crisis many workers have not been paid. These problems have not only reduced the region's attractiveness as a potential market but are actually encouraging people to leave the region entirely.

As noted above, this situation can only be aggravated by the current economic crisis, as the RFE is dependent upon goods imported from neighbouring countries. In fact the reliance upon foreign food imports has declined in recent years. In the mid-1990s Primorskii Krai imported 85 per cent of its food from abroad: in 1997 import dependence had declined to 60 per cent.[11] However, import dependence remains very high in the far north which is effectively cut off from Russian suppliers. At the same time, increased transportation costs will also make goods imported from elsewhere in Russia more expensive. Whatever the source of goods, the hard-pressed consumers find the purchasing power of their wages, if they are receiving wages, severely reduced by the devaluation of the rouble. Thus, workers in the RFE have gone from a privileged position during the Soviet period, when they received high wages and subsidies, to no wages, rapid inflation and a shortage of goods. It is no wonder that the authorities in Moscow are worried about civil unrest in Vladivostok and the local authorities are talking about issuing ration coupons again.

Demographic crisis

Between 1989 (the date of the last Soviet census) and the beginning of 1997 the population of the RFE declined from 7.941 million to 7.421 million (in 1990–91 it just reached eight million). Consequently, the region's share of Russia's population declined from 5.4 per cent in 1989 to 5.1 per cent at the beginning of 1997. This decline is due to both falling rates of natural increase (in 1989 there was a positive balance between births and deaths of 69,000, but in 1996 there were 17,000 more deaths than births), and out-migration. Rates of out-migration picked up in the early 1990s, but have declined more recently. Between 1989 and 1997 the region lost 646,000 people due to migration, and natural increase added 126,000, resulting in a net loss of 520,000 or 6.5 per cent of the 1989 population. As Table 4 reveals, there are substantial intraregional variations in population change.

Table 4: Population change in the Russian Far East, 1989–97

Region	Total population		Percentage change 1989–97			Absolute change 1989–97		
	1989	1997	Total	Natural	Migration	Total	Natural	Migration
Russia	14,7401	14,7501	0.1	-1.6	1.7	101	-2,409	2,510
RFE	7,941	7,421	-6.5	1.6	-8.1	-520	126	-646
Sakha	1,081	1,016	-6.0	7.0	-13.0	-65	76	-141
Primorskii	2,258	2,239	-0.9	0.1	-0.9	-19	2	-21
Khabarovsk	1,609	1,556	-3.3	0.4	-3.7	-54	6	-60
Jewish	216	207	-4.3	2.0	-6.3	-9	4	-14
Amur	1,058	1,032	-2.5	1.6	-4.1	-26	17	-43
Kamchatka	466	403	-13.6	1.6	-15.3	-64	8	-71
Koryak	39	33	-15.9	2.8	-18.7	-6	1	-7
Magadan	386	251	-34.9	1.8	-36.8	-135	7	-142
Chukotka	157	87	-44.3	4.0	48.3	-70	6	-76
Sakhalin	710	632	-11.0	0.0	-11.0	-78	0	-78

Source: T. Heleniak, 'Internal Migration in Russia During the Economic Transition', *Post-Soviet Geography and Economics*, Vol. 38, No. 2 (1997), p. 88.

Put simply, people have been leaving the northern regions in large numbers. For example, the current population of Magadan is 65 per cent of its 1989 level and that of Chukotka 55.4 per cent. In 1991 the northern regions of the RFE accounted for 26.3 per cent of the region's population, but at the beginning of 1997 the share of the north had declined to 23.7 per cent. This is dramatic proof of the collapse of the state-supported economies of these remote regions.

Further south the declines are less dramatic, though equally significant. This loss of population also reflects a drain on the region's human capital, as it is the younger, more able proportion of the workforce that is leaving. This also dampens down the rate of natural population growth and increases the dependency ratio. This is reflected in the ageing of the region's population. In 1989 the percentage of the RFE's population over working age was 10.4 per cent; at the beginning of 1997 it was 13.7 per cent.[12] The share under working age had declined from 28.1 per cent in 1989 to 23.9 per cent in 1997. Population projections produced by Timothy Heleniak at the World Bank suggest that by 2006 the region's population could fall below seven million. Projections produced by Goskomstat suggest a population of 6.8 million in 2005 and 6.6 million in 2010.[13] This contrasts with the current population of the neighbouring Chinese provinces of Heilonjiang, Jilin and Liaoning, which is greater than ninety million. Thus, the effective occupation of the RFE is increasingly recognized as a key issue for policy-makers in Moscow. At the same time local politicians are using xenophobic fears of uncontrolled Chinese immigration to justify increased federal spending.

Assessment

On balance, it is difficult to be optimistic about the current economic situation in the RFE. The region has been in crisis for at least ten years and the current economic crisis in Russia can only make a bad situation worse. No doubt there are many in the RFE who are wondering whether they would be better off outside the Russian Federation. The policies and false promises of the federal government have only served to aggravate the problems facing the region. To conclude this section, it is useful to look at the fundamentals of the economic situation in the RFE. The region's comparative advantage, at both a national and an international level, probably rests in the exploitation of its renewable and non-renewable resource bases. Two things are therefore required for the region to promote a resource-based economic recovery:

- capital investment to modernize the existing resource industries and develop new deposits and also to develop the infrastructure necessary to facilitate development and deliver commodities to market (in an ideal world additional investment would ensure that such developments were as environmentally friendly as possible); and

- markets that are willing to purchase the Far East's resource exports.

Thus, the very nature of the RFE as a resource periphery means that it is dependent upon the attitudes of those outside the region, both in Moscow and in Northeast Asia, as well as on the health of the global economy. An upturn in economic activity and a consequent increase in demand for the region's commodities would probably do more to promote economic recovery than any development programme proposed by Moscow. However, improved political relations between Moscow and the regions of the RFE would do much to encourage foreign investors to help develop the region's resources. The next chapter focuses upon the key internal and external political relationships that will shape the future for the RFE.

4 POLITICAL RELATIONS

As elsewhere in Russia, the collapse of the Soviet system of central control has resulted in the reconfiguration of political roles and relations, both between individual regions and the federal government in Moscow and between the various regions that comprise the RFE. Political relations are complicated by the fact that the RFE is a border region and plays a major role in Moscow's foreign policy towards the APR and more specifically China and Japan. Developments in the RFE are also an increasingly important component of Russian–US relations, principally through the activities of the Gore–Chernomyrdin Commission (subsequently the US–Russia Binational Commission). Thus, the political and geostrategic dimensions of development in the RFE are multi-layered and complex. The discussion below simplifies the situation by examining three scales of interaction: intraregional relations, relations between the RFE and Moscow and international relations.

Intraregional relations

The RFE as a political unit has no function – policy towards the region is the result of bilateral relations between Moscow and individual administrations. The current economic and political crisis in Russia has served to highlight the weakness of the federal government and has reopened debate about centre–region relations. So far, attempts to create a united front through the regional economic association (its full name is the Interregional Association for Economic Cooperation of the Russian Far East and Transbaykal Region) have failed for a number of reasons.

• First, the constituent regions enjoy different privileges and degrees of autonomy. Although the Russian Constitution states that all regions are equal, the
  reality is somewhat different. Russia's republics have seized more power and
  the Republic of Sakha (Yakutia) has been particularly aggressive in gaining
  increased autonomy. Equally, some of the region's lower-level autonomous
  regions, such as Chukotka, have broken away from the oblast administrations to
  which they were previously subordinate and now enjoy certain benefits because

15

of their autonomous standing. The net result is that the constituent regions of the RFE all have individual and differing relations with Moscow.

- Second, because the constituent regions face different problems they seek different things from the federal government. The plight of the regions of the north is very different from that of the southern ones. Energy-exporting regions such as Sakhalin have interests which differ from those of energy-importing regions such as Khabarovsk. Similarly, regions dependent upon border trade with China, such as Amur Oblast, have suffered from the tightening of the border regime orchestrated by Primorskii Krai. Such differences between regions make it difficult for the political leaders of the RFE to arrive at a unified set of demands.

- Third, the Soviet system created a high level of intraregional dependence, particularly in the fuels–energy complex. This has meant that the non-payments problems discussed above have been translated into intraregional payment problems. Thus, for example, Khabarovsk Krai owes Sakhalin hundreds of billions of roubles for non-payment of deliveries of oil and gas. Problems with the port infrastructure in Vladivostok and Nakhodka and on the Trans-Siberian railway undermine the economic effectiveness of the entire region. Thus, political problems in Primorskii Krai have a negative effect on the entire region.

- Finally, increasingly the regions see themselves in competition with one another for federal assistance and investment (both domestic and foreign). For example, there is now fierce rivalry between Khabarovsk and Vladivostok, with Khabarovsk marketing itself as the 'safe' place to establish a business in the RFE.

All of these factors, together with the lack of federal funding for the region's development programme, have resulted in a situation whereby individual administrations are seeking to devise and implement their own economic development strategies.[14] Given the level of interdependence bequeathed by the Soviet system and the nature of the regional economy, collective action would be far more effective. For example, the avoidance of duplication of effort and the promotion of specialization would result in more effective use of scarce capital. In the summer of 1997 the governors of Sakhalin, Khabarovsk and Primorskii signed an agreement to cooperate so as to maximize the local benefits of the Sakhalin oil and gas developments. However, during 1998 the governors of Khabarovsk and Sakhalin fell out over plans for the gasification of the RFE. The federal government supported Khabarovsk's view that the delivery of gas to the mainland should take precedence over piping gas to the south of Sakhalin.

Centre–periphery relations

This term is often used to describe issues affecting relations between the Russian federal government in Moscow (the centre) and the 89 federal subjects (the periphery). Central to this is the question of fiscal federalism, the division of responsibilities and revenues between the federal authorities and the local oblast-level administrations. Faced with declining revenues and pressure to stabilize budgetary expenditure, the federal authorities have devolved many functions to the local level. At the same time, the privatization of state-owned enterprises has resulted in the transfer of many welfare facilities and functions to the local administrations. The net result is that the local administrations have had to take on numerous additional responsibilities. However, the current tax regime and the collapse of economic activity have severely eroded the local tax base. Consequently, regional governors are continually lobbying Moscow for subsidies and are constantly adding local laws and taxes to an already excessive federal system. The situation in Moscow is complicated by differences between the government and the Duma. Local governors and oblast administrators travel to Moscow to lobby the Duma to pass legislation that would be beneficial to their region. The governors themselves are members of the Federation Council, but it is the party politics of the Duma that seems to dominate the legislative process. Consequently, major projects, such as the Sakhalin I and II oil and gas projects, are held hostage to the Duma's procrastination over production-sharing legislation. In fact most of the federal legislation governing resource development is problematic and acts as a major disincentive to would-be foreign investors in the RFE.

The situation is further aggravated by the failure of the federal government to pay its own employees in the regions and by the failure of federal organs, such as the armed forces, to pay for local services. In the RFE the situation is compounded by the severity of the economic crisis, by the high degree of reliance upon federal programmes, such as support for the Russian north, and by the extent of federal activity in the local regional economies. Individual regions have signed power-sharing agreements with Moscow and some have threatened to stop paying federal taxes, but the reality is that the RFE remains dependent upon Moscow. The administrative regions of the RFE are not particularly militant and there is little chance of an independent RFE – first, because it remains heavily dependent upon funds from Moscow; and, secondly, because owing to its strategic significance Moscow would not allow the region to go its own way. Rather, the failure of the Russian political system to create a working federalism and the current confusion over responsibility simply add to the problems confronting the region and erode the ability of local administrators to solve the problems they face. A foreign investor arriving in the region is often caught in a power-play between Moscow and the local administration.

Moreover, these same centre–region disputes often exist within regions, between the oblast administration, the city and the rayon/district administrations. The most notorious example of this is the long-running conflict between the governor of Primorskii Krai and the mayor of Vladivostok.[15]

International relations

These operate at two levels: at the local level between the regions of the RFE and neighbouring states and at the national level between Russia and the states of the APR (both multilaterally and bilaterally). The emphasis in the discussion that follows is upon the extent to which international political relations are promoting trade and investment.

Local networks

The oblast-level administrations The regionalization of the Russian economy and the expansion of foreign economic relations with the APR have created a new level of international interaction. The individual administrations in the region and the regional economic associations are pursuing bilateral links with key trading partners, namely China, Japan, South Korea and the United States. Various associations exist to promote trade and investment and some regions, such as the Republic of Sakha (Yakutia), have representative offices in Tokyo, for example. There is also cooperation between regional authorities, for example between Sakhalin Oblast and the State of Alaska and between Sakhalin and Hokkaido Prefecture in Japan.

Foreign actors At the same time, the 'opening up' of the RFE has allowed foreign organizations to set up operations in the region. There are consular operations for most of the major trade partners in Vladivostok. In November 1997 the Japanese government opened an office of its Khabarovsk Consulate in Yuzhno-Sakhalinsk. This was of symbolic significance because the disputed Kurile Islands or Northern Territories are administratively part of Sakhalin Oblast. The US Department of Commerce has sponsored the creation of a number of American business centres in the key administrative capitals. These are supposed to provide a 'home away from home' for US businesses prospecting in the Far East. The Japanese have also set up a series of Japan centres to provide language training and technical assistance for local businesses. The South Koreans are planning a business park in the port city of Nakhodka. A whole host of NGOs is now operational in the RFE as it becomes incorporated into global networks. Friends of the Earth (Tokyo) recently completed a major study of environmental problems in the RFE and has expressed concern about the environmental and social impacts of the Sakhalin oil and gas projects.[16]

Regionally targeted assistance   Finally, bilateral and multilateral organizations are adopting a more regional approach to financial and technical assistance. For Japan, South Korea and the United States the RFE is a priority region for their assistance programmes. The Gore–Chernomyrdin Commission chose the two regions of Khabarovsk and Sakhalin as part of its regional initiative programme. The other two regions in the project are Novgorod and Samara, both in European Russia. The European Bank for Reconstruction and Development (EBRD), in cooperation with Daiwa Securities, is running one of its regional venture capital funds out of Vladivostok. The Sakhalin II oil and gas project has obtained a loan from the EBRD to help fund phase one of its development.[17] The World Bank is involved in various resource-development and infrastructure projects. Finally, the United Nations is involved in trying to get the Tumen River project off the ground, although officials in Vladivostok see this project as competition for their own plans and have done little to promote it. Nonetheless, the RFE is now receiving direct assistance from foreign donors, although most of this support is within bilateral and multilateral agreements with Moscow. Moscow has stopped attempts by local political leaders to develop their own foreign policies towards the APR. Federal border guards and customs officers still control access to the region.

Interstate relations

During the Soviet period the superpower politics of the Cold War served to isolate the RFE from the APR. Most of the border and coastal regions were closed to foreign and Soviet citizens alike. Now the RFE is open, but many of the conflicts of the Cold War remain. For the RFE the key foreign actors are China, Japan, the United States and South Korea.

China

In the immediate post-Soviet period Russia struggled to devise a foreign policy that reflected its new-found role in the world. In September 1996 Russia signed a Strategic Partnership Agreement with China. This reflected the desire of both states to promote a multipolar world, to balance the effect of NATO expansion in Europe and to counter US dominance in the APR. However, so far at least, Russia has remained a relatively insignificant trading partner for China, whose open-door policy has focused on trade with Asia-Pacific and the United States and has benefited coastal regions rather than the northern interior. Nonetheless, at present China is an important trade partner for the RFE but is not a source of foreign capital. The northeastern regions of China that border the RFE are themselves relatively backward and seeking sources of investment and new markets. In fact the RFE may actually be in competition with China for certain types of investment.[18] For example, the abundance of cheap labour in China means that few foreign companies are likely to establish manufacturing activities in the RFE. China may yet prove to be a major market for resources from the RFE, especially oil and gas from Sakhalin and Sakha. At their summit meeting in November 1997, Russia and China announced their intention to develop gas deposits in Siberia to deliver gas to China. One of the projects, the Irkutsk project, also figured in the Yeltsin–Hashimoto summit. However, Russia's greatest concern must be the effective occupation of the territory of the RFE and what it perceives as extreme demographic pressure from northern China. The Beijing summit saw the signing of an agreement on border demarcation in the RFE; the agreement was criticized by local politicians in the RFE.

At present economic relations between Moscow and Beijing are focused on big-ticket items such as arms sales and nuclear plants, rather than border trade.[19] In recent years border trade has declined in significance, but it is possible that the current economic crisis in Russia will see the resumption of barter trade, as the Russian consumer can no longer afford to purchase higher-quality goods from Japan, South Korea and the United States. Nevertheless, uncontrolled large-scale movements of Chinese workers and traders into the RFE could quickly become a major source of tension.

Japan

Since the 1970s Japan has been involved in a number of large-scale investment projects in the RFE. At present, although Japanese business is highly visible in the RFE, the level of actual investment remains very modest. Japanese companies have been positioning themselves without making substantial commitments. This strategy makes sense: first, because the current investment environment in the RFE is too unstable to warrant large-scale investment (unless the Japanese government provides the funds); and, secondly, because the territorial dispute remains unresolved and is still a major barrier to increased investment. If either problem were solved then Japanese companies might be prepared to consider investment in the RFE. In other words, if the investment environment improved, Japanese companies would invest even if the territorial dispute remained unresolved.

However, the current state of the economy in the RFE and the economic situation in Japan make substantial investment extremely unlikely. At present, political relations between Moscow and Tokyo seem to be improving much faster than the investment climate in the RFE. Prime Minister Hashimoto's 'Eurasian Speech' in July 1996 laid the basis for a new policy towards relations with Russia. At the Yeltsin–Hashimoto summit in November 1997 in Krasnoyarsk, the Russian president and the Japanese prime minister announced their desire to resolve the territorial dispute by the year 2000. President Yeltsin visited Japan in the spring of 1998 and at a summit meeting at Kawana positive noises were made about the signing of a Peace and Friendship Treaty by the year 2000. Thus, a resolution to the territorial dispute appeared to be in sight.

Since then, however, Prime Minister Hashimoto has resigned and the new Japanese government under Prime Minister Keizo Obuchi has had to focus its efforts on Japan's domestic economic problems. Likewise, the Russian government has been concerned with domestic problems. Despite these problems, signs of progress on Sakhalin are attracting the interest of Japanese companies which are anxious to capture a large share of the contracts associated with the $25 billion oil and gas developments. However, Japan's involvement in the Sakhalin I project may be jeopardized by the economic problems facing the Japan National Oil Company. The state-owned company is the lead member of Sodeco, the consortium of Japanese companies involved in the Sakhalin I project.

Press statements following the Krasnoyarsk and Kawana summits suggested that the Japanese government was considering ways of providing further economic support for Russia's economic reforms and for the RFE in particular. As yet no concrete plans have been announced. Potential projects include the modernization of the Trans-Siberian railway, Sakhalin IV and V and the Irkutsk gas project. The Japanese Import-Export Bank was to provide Moscow with untied loans worth $800 million during 1998–99. However, the disbursement of these funds has been caught up in the economic crisis in Russia. One could suggest that, although political relations are showing signs of improvement, relatively few commercial opportunities exist for substantial Japanese investment in the RFE. An alternative strategy might be to provide funds to help realize the Federal Programme for the Development of the RFE and Transbaykal. However, such assistance would not be a commercial loan, but rather development assistance – a form of aid for which Russia does not currently qualify.

The United States

Increasingly strong links have been developing between Alaska and the Pacific Northwest and the RFE. In large part this is because of the West Coast Ad Hoc Working Group for US West Coast/Russian Far East Relations, which is part of the Gore–Chernomyrdin Commission. The primary motivation for these linkages is economic. The US government wishes to encourage US companies to invest in the resource industries of the RFE. Most of the major mining, oil and gas projects in the RFE involve US companies. In the case of Sakhalin, the US government wishes to make sure that US companies can compete with the Japanese for contracts related to oil and gas development. There is a strengthening West Coast/RFE network independent of linkages between Washington DC and Moscow. Obviously strategists in

Washington are well aware of the unstable nature of Northeast Asia and see economic recovery in the RFE as important to the maintenance of stability. Substantial commercial interests in the RFE also provide legitimacy to US diplomacy in the region. Equally, concerns over energy security mean that energy developments in the RFE (and Siberia) can help to reduce reliance upon the Middle East and also provide energy for China's booming economy.

In the post-Soviet era China, Japan, Russia and the United States have clearly emerged as the key political and economic actors in Northeast Asia. The current economic crisis in Russia has dealt a blow to those US businesses involved in trade with the region; however, US involvement in the Sakhalin projects is much more long-term and reflects a broader strategic vision of the role of the RFE in Northeast Asia. This does not mean that the Sakhalin projects are immune to the current turmoil. Should economic and political conditions continue to deteriorate in Russia and the Asian energy market remain depressed, it is possible that the Sakhalin projects would be put on hold. This would be a major blow for the RFE.

South Korea

As latecomers to the RFE, South Korean companies were faced with a steep learning curve and many have made costly mistakes.[20] In the late 1980s Seoul hoped that Moscow could be persuaded to adopt a more balanced approach to the situation on the Korean peninsula. South Korea provided credits worth $3 billion to fund trade with the Soviet Union. When the Soviet Union collapsed this credit was extended to Russia. Now it is a major obstacle to the expansion of trade relations as Russia is having problems repaying the loan. South Korean companies see the former Soviet Union as a market, as a source of raw materials, as a source of research and development capacity and even as a place to produce. The RFE was clearly seen as a source of raw materials and various South Korean companies have been involved in resource-development projects in the region (as well as in East Siberia). In 1996, 58.2 per cent of South Korean investment in Russia went to the RFE and a further 30.9 per cent went to Moscow. However, South Korean corporations lack the experience of the Japanese of working in the RFE and also lack the technical expertise of US companies of operating in harsh environmental conditions. Consequently, there has been more talk than action when it comes to South Korean investment in the RFE.

At present South Korean investment activity in the region is rather modest and in decline. Among South Korea's large trading companies (*chaebols*), only Hyundai has made significant investments in the region. Hyundai's Svetlaya forestry project has been a complete disaster, attracting adverse publicity on environmental grounds and failing to meet its commercial objectives. Consequently the project was finally liquidated in 1998. In the autumn of 1997 Hyundai opened a $100 million hotel and business complex in Vladivostok, but the project has suffered from heavy taxation by the federal government. The plight of the Korean Land Corporation's Nakhodka business park is symptomatic of the problems facing Korean investors. The business park is the result of an intergovernmental agreement between Seoul and Moscow, but its development has been plagued by delays. It has yet to break ground and is now having major problems finding tenants. Initially, the park was to cater for Russian and Korean companies and Russian–Korean joint ventures; however, a lack of interest means that the park is seeking to attract clients from wherever possible.

In addition to problems in the RFE itself, domestic economic problems and the prospects of unification have resulted in a more cautious approach to investment in the RFE. Given that the financial crisis that hit South Korea in late 1997 forced the *chaebols* to reconsider investments in the European Union, it is a certainty that risky projects in the RFE are no longer on the agenda. A case in point is Hanbo Steel, which is faced with bankruptcy. A subsidiary of Hanbo had a substantial share of the Irkutsk gas project, but sold most of its interest to the Russian oil company Sidanko. Sidanko then sold part of its share to British Petroleum. This has left South Korea with a modest 7 per cent interest in what promises to be a major gas project and a focus of Russian–Chinese energy relations. Finally, even if there were good opportunities to be had in the RFE, South Korean companies would face stiff competition from Japanese and US companies.

Although it is safe to assume that South Korean companies are not going to invest substantial sums in the RFE, they are still very interested in trading with the region. South Korea's trade with Russia and the RFE has grown despite the bad experience of direct investment. While the Asian crisis may have actually enhanced South Korea's role as a source of imported consumer goods, the crash of the rouble may now price South Korean goods out of the domestic market.

Multilateral organizations

A final aspect of the international scene is Russian involvement in multilateral organizations in the Northeast Asian and Asia-Pacific region. Russia has shown a strong desire to form closer associations with organizations such as ASEAN (the Association of Southeast Asian Nations) and has sought to join various regional institutions such as the Asian Development Bank and APEC (Asia-Pacific Economic Cooperation). Russia's recent attempts to join APEC had been thwarted on the grounds that although Russia was part of the APR, its economic core lay to the west of the Urals in Europe. However, at the Krasnoyarsk summit the Japanese government agreed to support Russia's application to APEC. In return, Russia agreed to support Japan's claim to a permanent seat on the UN Security Council. In late November 1997, at the Vancouver summit, Russia was admitted as a member of APEC. Clearly, if Russia is to be accepted as part of the Asia-Pacific community it must first effectively develop the RFE. Only then will more substantial economic ties with the region develop. Integration into the APR will be made possible by the economic development of the RFE but it is not a panacea for the problems that face the RFE.[21] In summary, politicians in the RFE and Moscow would do well to focus on the bilateral relations that will help promote the economic development of the RFE and this in turn will result in a greater legitimacy for Russia's claims to be a Pacific state.

5 THE ROLE OF FOREIGN TRADE AND INVESTMENT

As noted above, the RFE was the only region in the Soviet Union where the expansion of export-oriented economic activity was an accepted development strategy. However, this strategy was orchestrated through the central planning system and the state monopoly over foreign trade. Only a very small share of foreign trade was controlled locally. During the Soviet period Moscow controlled the RFE's economic interaction, and foreign economic relations served the Soviet Union's interests rather than the needs of the regional economy.[22] The emphasis was upon the sale of raw materials to Japan to finance the import of machinery and equipment. However, the expansion of Soviet trade with the Asia-Pacific region during this period was predominantly in the form of economic assistance for client states. This trade was dominated by the supply of oil, machinery, equipment and armaments (it is noteworthy that in 1996 the RFE's major export earner was the sale of MIG fighter aircraft constructed in Khabarovsk Krai). The RFE did not play a significant role in this trade and by the mid-1980s the region accounted for only 28 per cent of the Soviet Union's trade with the APR.

During the late Soviet period reforms introduced as part of perestroika created new forms of cooperation between Soviet enterprises and foreign companies, and also promoted the increasing decentralization and regionalization of control over foreign trade and investment. These processes were accelerated by the collapse of the Soviet Union, with the result that control over foreign trade between enterprises in the RFE and the APR now resides in the region and the foreign trade regime is managed by the local administrations. The net result has been that Russia's trade with the APR principally involves the RFE and also that the commodity structure of that trade more closely reflects the needs of the region. However, it would be wrong to think that Moscow no longer has a part to play. The legal and fiscal regulations relating to foreign trade are set in Moscow and customs remains a federal responsibility.

Recent developments

Over the past decade there have been a number of new developments in the sphere of foreign economic relations.

Table 5: Russian foreign trade with major partners in Northeast Asia ($US billion)

Country	1993	1994	1995	1996	1997
China	7.68	5.08	5.46	6.85	6.12
Japan	4.27	4.66	5.93	4.95	5.01
South Korea	1.58	2.19	3.31	3.78	3.30

Source: *Russian Review*, Vol. 5, No. 12 (1998), p. 25.

Increased dependence upon foreign trade activity

To compensate for the distancing of the RFE from traditional suppliers in the European regions of the former Soviet Union, there has been an increased reliance on the import of food products, consumer goods etc. from the APR (as well as second-hand cars from Japan). In 1996, to compensate for the failure of domestic suppliers, Chukotka imported oil and oil products from the United States. The breakdown of internal linkages has forced these more remote regions to become increasingly dependent on foreign suppliers. In regions such as Magadan and Kamchatka, US companies have become major suppliers of foodstuffs. In general, imports to the RFE have been financed by the export of raw materials, but the region now faces an increasing balance-of-payments problem as import demand outstrips present export potential. This problem can only be aggravated by the collapse of the rouble.

Exports from the RFE are predominantly fish and fish products, fuels, minerals (including diamonds) and metals (including gold), timber and timber products and arms (MIG aircraft). There is marked regional variation in the reliance of industry upon export markets, the major exporting regions being Sakhalin, Primorskii and Khabarovsk. As domestic demand has fallen, an increasing share of the region's production has gone to export. The balance-of-payments problem is aggravated by the fact that a large percentage of the region's export earnings are kept offshore. For example, fish are commonly sold to foreign processing ships on the high seas and, like the fish, the cash from such sales never lands in the Far East.

Boom and bust in Chinese–Russian border trade

In the early post-Soviet period Chinese border trade played a major part in the expansion of foreign trade in the region. However, this initial boom has been followed by a substantial reduction in trade volumes – first, because the small size of the market in the RFE and its limited purchasing power have resulted in the rapid saturation of the local markets; and, second, because Russian concerns about large-scale Chinese migration into the region have resulted in the tightening of border controls and the increased monitoring of border trade activities. Russian business in the region also claims that the influx of poor-quality products from China is repressing the development of Russian businesses. It is clear that border trade can do little to solve the structural problems facing the RFE. However, such trade provides an important source of food products and consumer goods for the region. As noted above, the current economic crisis in Russia may actually promote a growth of border trade. On the other hand, many Chinese traders prefer to convert their rouble profits into US dollars before returning to China. Thus, the devaluation of the rouble may threaten the profitability of such shuttle trade.

Emergence of new trading partners

During the Soviet period, trade with the APR was dominated by fledgling socialist states in the region. Now trade is based on economics rather than ideology and new trading partners have emerged. Today four trade partners dominate the RFE's economic relations with the APR: China, Japan, South Korea and the United States. In 1996 these four countries accounted for 74.4 per cent of the foreign trade turnover of the RFE (see Table 6). Most recently, Australia and New Zealand have emerged as suppliers of foodstuffs, but the inability of traders in the RFE to pay for imports has created problems. While China has been a major trade partner, it is not a source of foreign investment. Japan, South Korea and the United States dominate foreign investment and joint-venture activity.

Table 6: Geographical distribution of foreign trade activity in the Russian Far East in 1996 ($US million)

	Total	%	Exports	%	Imports	%	Balance
China	955	24.3	747	33.2	208	12.4	539
Japan	883	22.5	737	32.8	146	8.7	591
Korea	612	15.6	334	14.8	278	16.5	56
US	470	12.0	45	2.0	425	25.3	-380
FSU	129	3.3	25	1.1	104	6.2	-79
Other	884	22.5	362	16.1	522	31.0	-160
Total	3,933	100	2,250	100	1,683	100	567

Source: Russian Far East Update, October (1997), p. 15.

Table 7: Foreign trade activity in the RFE in 1996 ($US '000)

	Total	%	Exports	%	Imports	%	Balance
Sakha	425,247.8	10.9	227,840.6	10.1	197,407.2	12.1	30,433.4
Jewish	10,234.7	0.3	5,326.7	0.2	4,908.1	0.3	418.6
Chukotka	15,756.9	0.4	44.2	0.0	15,712.8	1.0	−15,668.6
Primorskii	1,230,503.2	31.6	600,811.9	26.7	629,691.3	38.4	−28,879.4
Khabarovsk	1,075,842.7	27.7	829,396.9	36.9	246,445.8	15.0	582,951.1
Amur	98,260.6	2.5	46,028.5	2.0	52,232.1	3.2	−6,203.6
Kamchatka	323,032.4	8.3	172,544.6	7.7	150,487.8	9.2	22,056.8
Magadan	148,794.9	3.8	21,533.4	1.0	127,261.5	7.8	−105,728.1
Sakhalin	560,333.4	14.4	346,652.6	15.4	213,680.8	13.0	132,971.8
Total RFE	3,888,006.6	100	2,250,179.4	100	1,637,827.4	100	612,352.0

Source: *Russian Far East Update*, July (1997), p. 15.

A clear coastal and border orientation to foreign economic activity

The expansion of foreign trade and investment activity has a distinct geography. Foreign traders and investors are nudging nervously into the region, preferring to trade in the coastal and border regions. This is largely due to the region's inadequate infrastructure. In 1996 the three coastal regions of Khabarovsk, Primorskii and Sakhalin accounted for 73.7 per cent of the region's foreign trade turnover (Table 7).[23] However, the foreign trade activity of the northern regions, particularly the Republic

Table 8: Foreign investment activity in 1997

	Number of enterprises with foreign participation	Average number of workers per enterprise	Exports ($US million)	Imports ($US million)	Foreign investment in 1997 ($US '000)	Cumulative per capita FDI at end of 1997 ($US)
Russia	14,734	467.3	6,453	6,244	3,897,357	84.9
Far East	716	20.9	199.4	125.1	14,0195	128.2
Sakha	30	0.7	12.2	0.2	9,789	36.4
Jewish	8	0.02	0	0.01	439	836.1
Primorskii	323	8.3	66.9	73.7	9,953	51.1
Khabarovsk	140	6	51.7	10.6	10,469	103.6
Amur	63	1	4.7	9.2	239	77.5
Kamchatka	41	1.2	7.5	5.3	832	118.2
Koryak	2	0.1	0	0	–	–
Magadan	22	0.6	5.5	2.8	61,610	721.2
Sakhalin	89	3.1	50.9	23.3	46,864	247.7
RFE as % of Russia	4.9	–	3.1	2.0	3.6	–

Source: *Goskomstat Rossii*, various publications.

Table 9: Barriers to foreign investment in the RFE

American Chamber of Commerce	East Asian Analytical Unit
Deficiencies in the existing taxation system	Political uncertainty
Customs regulation issues	High inflation and shaky currency
Crime and corruption	Decline of domestic investment and run-down capital stock
Access to sources of financing	Inconsistent and unpredictable investment legislation
Shortage of skilled personnel	
Problems of the indigenous population	High tariffs and taxes
Transportation issues	High level of loss-making enterprises and the preference of management for the 'second option' in privatization (where a controlling package of shares is held by the enterprise collective)
Telecommunication issues	
Under-developed social infrastructure	
Freedom of movement and consular services	
Establishment of free economic zones	

Sources: American Chamber of Commerce in Russia, *White Paper: Economic Cooperation between the Russian Far East and the US West Coast and Alaska* (Moscow: American Chamber of Commerce in Russia, 1996); and East Asian Analytical Unit, *Pacific Russia: Risks and Rewards* (Canberra: EAAU, Department of Foreign Affairs and Trade, 1996).

of Sakha (Yakutia) are depressed by the omission of revenues of gold and diamond exports which are controlled by Moscow and do not appear in the regional foreign trade statistics. Within most of the regions, trade and investment activity is concentrated in the administrative capitals. Thus, increased integration with APR is likely to concentrate economic activity further in the southern coastal regions.

Despite the expansion of foreign trade and the emergence of new trade partners, the scale of foreign investment in the RFE remains modest (see Table 8). In fact the region's share of joint ventures has actually fallen as Moscow and European Russia had benefited from market-oriented investments. In many instances the initial allure of the region's wealth has been tarnished by the realities of doing business in Russia's 'wild east'. At the end of 1996 the cumulative stock of FDI in the region was US$811 million. Admittedly, there are substantial investments planned in the mining industry in the far north and in oil and gas development offshore of Sakhalin. But there are also numerous disaster stories, such as Hyundai's ill-fated Svetlaya forestry project. Many of the problems that are discouraging foreign investors originate in Moscow, particularly the chaotic legal system, the confiscatory tax regime and the failure to pass production-sharing legislation. However, these problems are often aggravated by the actions of local administrations and by organized crime. At the same time the region's poor infrastructure adds cost to even the most basic business transaction. Table 9 lists the various barriers to investment identified by foreign companies trying to do business in the RFE. Many of these problems are common to all regions in Russia; however, there is a perception that they are particularly acute in the RFE.

The bottom line is that the collapse of the Soviet Union and the regionalization of economic activity have created new opportunities for trade between the RFE and the APR, but current conditions in the region are limiting the potential for export-based economic development. Even with an improved investment environment, the small size of the regional market and the lack of infrastructure will serve to focus activity on the port cities and administrative capitals of the southern regions.

6 PROSPECTS FOR THE NEW MILLENNIUM

This final chapter presents a number of scenarios to explore the possible future development of the Russian Far East. Mention has already been made of the Federal Programme for the Economic and Social Development of the Far East and the Transbaykal for 1996–2005. This document is a major policy statement about the future economic development strategy for the RFE. The period 1996–2000 is identified as one of stabilization during which economic decline ends and the preconditions for recovery are created. The period 2000–2005 is seen as the timescale for economic recovery. The programme presents a solid analysis of the problems facing the region, but fails to explain adequately how the funds will be found and how and by whom the plan should be implemented. For the purposes of the current analysis it is important to note that according to the Federal Programme economic recovery will be based on two factors:

- The Russian Far East and the Transbaykal currently and in the future represent one of the largest remaining resource bases in Russia. That natural resource potential can be used to meet the needs of the economy and also to generate income from exports for both the federal and regional budgets.
- The 'economic geographic position', including the border-coastal location, is favourable for the development of economic relations with the countries of the Asia-Pacific region. This factor can compensate for the distance of the region from the Russian market and increasing transportation costs.

Key determinants of growth

What factors are critical to the success of this export-based development strategy?

The national economic situation

Despite being distant from the domestic market, the RFE is heavily dependent upon support from the federal government. Only economic recovery will enable the federal government to meet its financial obligations in the region and even to allow more substantial funds to be allocated to the development programme.

The foreign trade regime

A more open economy and an improved environment for foreign investors are critical to the future of the RFE. In large part it is the federal government and Duma in Moscow that set the legislation framework for foreign investors. At the same time local administrators in the RFE could do much more to attract foreign investment. The RFE is only just waking up to the fact that in the era of globalization capital is footloose and no one will invest in the RFE unless they can gain a return on their investment (this is particularly true of private Russian investors).

International commodity and financial markets

As a resource-exporting region, the RFE is vulnerable to the boom and bust cycles of supply and demand. In international terms, the region is likely to be a 'high-cost' producer and thus particularly susceptible to price fluctuations. Continued economic growth in the APR is essential to provide a market for the RFE's resources, but the RFE will continue to face stiff competition from other suppliers. There is no guarantee of access to markets at prices that will return a profit. Cooperation with foreign multinational corporations with marketing experience will make gaining a foothold in new markets much easier.

Intraregional cooperation

It is essential that the regions that comprise the RFE learn to work together to expand their economic relations with the APR. At one level they are in competition; however, they are also dependent upon one another. In a context where the federal government has limited funds, local cooperation in the pursuit of an export-oriented development strategy will benefit the entire region. For example, the port cities are dependent upon freight generated in their hinterlands. At the same time, plans for industrial restructuring aim to reorient industry in the south to the needs of the resource industries in the north and offshore. No region can go it alone.

Centre–periphery relations

Just as intraregional cooperation is required, a clear demarcation of responsibilities and revenues between the federal government and the oblast-level administrative units is also needed. At present the local state cannot sustain the increased burden that has been placed upon it by the federal centre. The current asymmetries between the republics and the rest are divisive and serve to undermine the federal system.

Given the importance attached to increased integration with the states of the APR, positive political relations are essential. Moscow needs to create a constructive environment within which local contacts can flourish. Neither the policy-makers in Moscow nor the local politicians in the RFE can develop relations independent of one another. Russia's foreign policy in the region shapes what is possible at the local level, but developments at the local level can serve to reinforce and promote good relations. Russia must accept that its involvement in the APR is likely to be judged by its economic performance and not the extent of its firepower, which is just as well given the current state of the Pacific Fleet!

Scenarios

Three scenarios are presented below in tabular form:

'*Boom*' which represents the successful pursuit of a resource-based, export-oriented development strategy and increased integration with the APR;

'*Muddling through*' which represents a continuation of the present situation with the RFE failing to develop its export potential but managing to avoid further economic decline; and

'*Bust*' which represents further economic decline, the collapse of the region's economy and increased isolation from the APR.

Table 10: Scenarios for the future development of the RFE

Boom	Muddling through	Bust
National economic situation		
Slow and steady economic recovery. Effective economic restructuring and the growth of new sectors and regions.	A 'bottoming out' of economic decline with selective economic recovery. Limited signs of new economic growth which is highly selective in terms of branches and regions of the economy.	Continued economic depression, prolonged payments problems, little effective restructuring, continued reliance upon resource exports and failing federal subsidies.

Boom	Muddling through	Bust
Foreign trade regime		
Open economy with a coherent and transparent foreign trade and investment regime that protects the right of investors. Domestic enterprises encouraged to participate in foreign trade. Membership of WTO etc.	Ambivalent attitude towards foreign investment (FI), failure to create an attractive environment for FDI. FI restricted to a small number of large resource and manufacturing projects involving major MNCs. Protracted negotiations over WTO membership.	Closed economy, hostile to FI. Re-imposition of state control over foreign trade. Increased protectionism and import substitution. Failure to join WTO.
International commodity markets		
Continued economic growth in the APR and the emergence of China as a new market create new opportunities for resource exports from RFE. MNCs attracted to FDI in both resource production and primary processing.	Selected opportunities remain as a supplier of 'unprocessed' raw materials. Limited FDI in new projects, but emphasis on production rather than processing.	Recession in the APR and increased competition squeezes the RFE out of resource markets. Depressed prices reduce profitability of exports. Little interest from MNCs in developing resource potential of RFE.
Intraregional cooperation		
Economic recovery provides a solution to the non-payments problems. Effective cooperation with joint development of infrastructure and agreement on intraregional specialization. The regional economic association presents a united front to Moscow and potential investors.	Continued reliance upon the federal centre to resolve non-payments problems. Limited cooperation on mega-projects, such as Sakhalin oil and gas. The regional economic association remains little more than a 'talking shop'.	Increased conflict and rivalry between regions, no resolution of the non-payments problem, duplication of infrastructure problems with investors able to play one region off against another. The regional economic association collapses.

Boom	Muddling through	Bust
	Centre–periphery relations	
Clear demarcation of revenues and responsibilities between the centre and the regions through a functioning federal system. Increased cooperation between the regions and the centre. The federal government shows a strong commitment, backed up by funds, to implement the programme for the RFE and Transbaykal.	Continued lack of clarity between the centre and the regions. Individual regions continue to make special deal with the federal government. Crisis management response by the federal government to problems as and where they arise. The federal government fails to provide funds to implement the programme for the RFE and Transbaykal.	Increased conflict between the centre and the regions, non-payment of federal taxes causes fiscal crisis and the collapse of the federal system. Regions left to fend for themselves on the basis of the financial resources at hand. Federal government abdicates responsibility for resolving regional problems and the Federal Programme for RFE and Transbaykal is forgotten.
	Political relations with the APR	
Resolution of the territorial conflict results in substantial Japanese government assistance and an influx of Japanese FDI in the RFE. Financial problems with South Korea are resolved and Russia supports unification. Energy supplies from the RFE play a major role in improved relations between China and Russia. Fearing a loss of opportunity, the United States steps up support for US companies investing in the RFE. Substantial FDI and foreign trade with APR and increased integration of Northeast Asia.	No resolution of the territorial dispute with Japan, just an agreement to disagree. Financial problems sour relations with South Korea. Relations with China pay scant attention to events in the RFE as China rejects the idea of relying upon imported energy. The United States judges economic support on purely financial grounds. The RFE fails to develop effective economic linkages with the APR.	Breakdown of discussion about the territorial dispute with Japan. Russian support for North Korea alienates South Korea. Increased illegal Chinese immigration in the RFE triggers border disputes. The United States withdraws financial and technical support because of increasing nationalist policies and the failure of market reforms. The disengagement of the RFE from the APR.

Consequences

This section summarizes the potential consequences for the RFE of the boom and bust scenarios presented above. This appraisal explores four dimensions of the future development of the RFE: the economy, the level of equality (within the region and in relation to Russia), the demographic situation, and international relations.

Boom

Economy: Successful economic recovery based on the expansion of resource exports to the APR, together with substantial FDI and the development of resource-processing industries.

Equality: Economic growth is concentrated in the southern border and coastal regions, but the closure of many northern settlements and the movement of people to the south reduce levels of inequality within the region. Socio-economic indicators in the south of the region are well above the national average, but the north requires substantial federal support to sustain its social infrastructure.

Demography: New employment opportunities and improving standards of living stabilize the population in the south and attract new workers to the region. The spatial redistribution of the population ensures the effective occupation of those regions bordering China. The emptying of the north is unavoidable, but creates major social and cultural problems for the indigenous populations that remain.

International relations: Economic recovery brings with it new linkages with neighbours in Northeast Asia and the Asia-Pacific region more generally. The RFE is widely accepted as part of Asia-Pacific, and the growth of Vladivostok to rival cities such as Vancouver, Seattle and Sydney is symbolic of the region's new status.

Bust

Economy: Continued economic decline and depression result in the collapse of the region's economy; only isolated mining and forestry projects remain profitable, the manufacturing and food processing industries in the south cease to function and the energy system falls into disrepair. Foreign investors stay away and only the fishing industry is able to maintain foreign trade activity, but this is largely offshore.

Equality: Those sub-regions that have resources are relatively prosperous, but most of the RFE is severely depressed; socio-economic indicators for the majority of the administrative regions are substantially below the Russian average and the entire region requires federal support.

Demography: The population of the RFE continues to decline, not just in the north, but also in the major cities of the south. The loss of younger and more able people aggravates the growing labour shortages and creates an increasingly elderly and dependent population. Increased immigration from China results in and causes tensions.

International relations: The 'ineffective occupation' of the RFE causes problems for Moscow and influences its foreign policy towards the APR. Increased isolation and the development of a siege mentality spark conflicts on the border with China and in territorial waters where foreign fishing boats encroach. Moscow is driven to strengthen its borders and finance the modernization of its forces in the RFE. This time the emphasis is upon protecting territorial integrity rather than upon power projection into the Pacific. The material and moral collapse of Vladivostok, despite increased military expenditure, is symbolic of Russia's failure to benefit from the dawn of the 'Pacific Century'.

Conclusions

So where is the RFE now? When this scenario-building exercise began in the autumn of 1997, I was persuaded to be optimistic in my assessment of the situation and concluded that the region was on the positive side of 'muddling through'. Since then four interrelated events have forced me to be more pessimistic: the Asian financial crisis, the decline in energy prices, the Russian economic crisis and the seeming inability of the new Russian government to come up with a strategy for dealing with the situation. As I read through the economic dimensions of the bust scenario it all seems horribly familiar. What remains to be seen is whether or not Russia will adopt a more introspective and/or combative foreign policy as a consequence of the current crisis.

The fact that less than a year has seen a dramatic change in the fortunes of the RFE is clear evidence of how vulnerable the region is. On the face of it the economic situation there was no worse in mid-1998 than it was in mid-1997: in fact there were positive signs. However, as a dependent resource periphery the region relies upon continued economic support from Moscow on the one hand, and foreign trade and investment from the APR on the other. The combination of the Asian crisis and then the Russian crisis has dealt the region a double blow. It would seem that there is little that the region can do itself to improve its situation in the short term. Greater cooperation between the administrative regions and a clamp-down on crime and corruption would surely help make the RFE a better place to invest in and trade with. However, only economic recovery in Asia and sound management in Moscow will create the conditions in which the region can realize its potential.

NOTES

1 For recent analyses of developments in the Russian Far East see: T. Akaha (ed.), *Politics and Economics in the Russian Far East: Changing Ties with Asia-Pacific* (London: Routledge, 1997), and M. J. Valencia (ed.), *The Russian Far East in Transition: Opportunities for Regional Economic Cooperation* (Boulder: Westview Press, 1995). In addition the journal *Transition* carried a special feature on the Russian Far East in its edition of 8 September 1995.

2 According to V.I. Ivanov et al., in 1996 4.7 trillion roubles, about 13% of the funds required by the programme, were allocated to its projects. In 1997 the federal government allocated a mere 1.034 trillion of the 40.5 trillion roubles requested by the region (*ERINA Report*, No. 23, 1997, pp. 39–40).

3 E. Miller and S. Stefanopoulos (eds), *The Russian Far East: A Business Reference Guide* (Seattle: Russian Far East Update, 1997), pp. 122–3.

4 L. Dienes, 'Economic and Strategic Position of the Soviet Far East: Development and Prospect', in A. Rodgers (ed.), *The Soviet Far East: Geographical Perspectives on Development* (London: Routledge, 1990), pp. 269–301.

5 L. Dienes, 'The Development of Siberian Regions: Economic Profiles, Income Flows and Strategies for Growth', *Soviet Geography*, Vol. 23, No. 4 (1982), pp. 205–44.

6 M. J. Bradshaw, 'Soviet Asian-Pacific Trade and the Regional Development of the Soviet Far East', *Soviet Geography*, Vol. 29, No. 4 (1988), pp. 367–93.

7 M. J. Bradshaw, 'Trade and High Technology' in R. Swearingen (ed.), *Siberia and the Far East: Strategic Dimensions in International Perspective* (Stanford: Hoover Institution Press, 1988), pp. 100–34.

8 P. A. Minakir and G. L. Freeze, *The Russian Far East: An Economic Survey* (2nd edition) (RIOTP: Khabarovsk, 1996), p. 13.

9 East Asian Analytical Unit, *Pacific Russia: Risks and Rewards* (EAAU: Canberra, 1996), p. 1. This study provides a very down-to-earth assessment of the prospects for the RFR and the problems foreign investors face.

10 M. J. Bradshaw and P. Kirkow, 'The Energy Crisis in the Russian Far East: Origins and Solutions', *Europe-Asia Studies*, Vol. 50, No. 6 (1998), pp. 1043–63.

11 *Russian Far East Update* (1998), September, p. 8. For a more detailed analysis of the food situation in the RFE see: V. Tikhomirov, 'Food Balance in the Russian Far East', *Polar Geography*, Vol. 21, No. 3 (1997), pp. 155–202.

12 Minakir and Freeze, p. 382, and Goskomstat Rossii, *Demographic Yearbook of Russia 1997* (Moscow: Goskomstat, 1997), p. 46.

13 *Demographic Yearbook of Russia* (1997), p. 552.

14 For example, the governor of Khabarovsk Krai, Viktor Ishaev, has published a book about the economic situation in Khabarovsk: V. Ishaev, *Ekonomicheskaya Reforms v Regione: tendenstii razvitiya i regulirovaniye* (Vladivostok: Dalnauka, 1998). In summer 1998 the Sakhalin administration commissioned an Alaska-based consulting company, Northern Economics, to produce an infrastructure development strategy for the island. The project was funded by USAID and the oil companies involved in the Sakhalin projects.

15 See: P. Kirkow, 'Regional Warlordism in Russia: the Case of Primorskii Krai', *Europe-Asia Studies*, Vol. 47, No. 6 (1995), pp. 923–47, and T. Troyakova, 'Regional Policy in the Russian Far East and the Rise of Localism in Primorye', *The Journal of East Asian Affairs*, Vol. 9, No. 2 (1995), pp. 428–61.

16 Friends of the Earth International, *Hotspots in the Russian Far East*. Environmental groups also lobbied the EBRD to try to stop it funding phase one development of the Sakhalin II project. For further discussion of the environmental dimensions of the Sakhalin projects see: *Pacific Oil and Gas Report*, Vol. 1. No. 1 (1998), pp. 1 and 8.

17 Phase one involves the development of so-called 'early oil'. An oil production platform was put in place in autumn 1998 and first production is expected in early summer 1999.

18 D. Kerr, 'China's Relations with the Russian Far East', paper prepared for the Russian Far East seminar held at Chatham House, 18 September 1998. A paper on this topic is also forthcoming in *Europe-Asia Studies*.

19 See: D. Kerr, 'Opening and Closing the Sino-Russian Border Trade: Regional Development and Political Interests in Northeast Asia', *Europe-Asia Studies*, Vol. 48, No. 6 (1996), pp. 931–58.

20 See: C.B. Lee and M. J. Bradshaw, 'Politics Versus Economics: The Changing Fortunes of South Korean–Russian Economic Relations', *Post-Soviet Geography and Economics*, Vol. 38, No. 8 (1997), pp. 461–77.

21 For an excellent assessment of the various plans to promote economic integration in Northeast Asia see: G. Rozman, 'Flawed Regionalism: Reconceptualizing Northeast Asia in the 1990s', *The Pacific Review*, Vol. 11, No. 1 (1998), pp. 1–27.

22 For a discussion of trade relations between the Soviet Far East and the APR see: M.J. Bradshaw, 'Soviet Asian-Pacific Trade and the Regional Development of the Soviet Far East', *Soviet Geography*, Vol. 29, No. 4 (1988), pp. 367–93, and G. Segal, *The Soviet Union and the Pacific* (London: RIIA/Unwin Hyman, 1990).

23 All data on foreign trade and investment activity should be treated with extreme caution. Large amounts of trade go unreported and data for foreign investment are often inflated by the inclusion of loans. The high level of shuttle trade is one reason for under-reporting, and another is the omission of gold and diamond exports from the regional trade figures. It is safe to assume that there are larger amounts of money and goods circulating in the region's economy than is suggested by the official figures.

THE ROYAL INSTITUTE OF INTERNATIONAL AFFAIRS

Chatham House 10 St James's Square London SW1Y 4LE Telephone **0171 957 5700** Fax 0171 957 5710